Life and Afterlife, Q&A
By Dr. Robert Kandarjian DC

***

Also by author:
Sacred Intentions
The Masculine Heart
Little Heroes (a children's book)
The Living and the Dead
Dream Ice Cream

Copyright © 2009 Dr. Robert Kandarjian DC
Second Edition 2023
All rights reserved.
ISBN: 1-4392-3049-8
ISBN-13: 9781439230497
Visit www.Amazon.com to order additional copies.

"Seek Divine Wealth"

Lahiri Mahasaya

CHAPTERS

Introduction……………...……………………..……….viii

1. I always seem to attract relationships that are unhealthy and sometimes abusive. What do I need to change? 1

2. I find myself having a very hard time forgiving myself because I feel I should be a better mother to my three kids and I'm not always a good mother. 4

3. I've been a heavy smoker since I was in my 20's and I now have lung cancer. How can I use my free will to heal myself? 7

4. If I was a king in my last life, why do I have to work at a gas station? 10

5. My mother died of cancer two years ago and I feel her around me especially at work. I feel that she's protecting me, but I also feel she isn't at peace with herself. 13

6. Whenever I talk to my teenage daughter it seems we always end up in an argument or a fight. What can we do to get along and have more peace? 16

7. How does long-distance healing work when someone is thousands of miles away? 19

8. How do I know what I should pursue in college and if the career I want is for my highest good? 22

9. Can energy healing help my children and how often would they need healing? 25

10. Can people be obsessed by evil spirits and negative energy and how can we protect ourselves? 28

11. What if a negative energy doesn't want to go to the Light? 31

12. Do we have to come back to earth to complete our healing and learning process or can we do it on the other side? 34

13. What happens to us after we die? 37

14. What happens to a person who commits suicide? 40

15. How do you define what a spiritual life is? 43

16. Are some children born with more spirituality than others? 46

17. When I'm trying to decide something important how do I know I'm making the right decision? 49

18. Does prayer work and can God give me what I pray for? 52

19. What is the afterlife like? 55

20. How can we get in touch with our intuitive side? 58

21. I am married to someone who refuses to be accountable and tries to always convince me that I am the one who needs to change. He won't go to counseling with me and after 12 years I don't know what my next move should be. 61

22. What is the best way to control and stop evil? 64

23. Do I need to belong to a religion to live a spiritual life? 67

24. My father is in his 80's and has been very sick for over a year. He is near death but has a strong will and fights every day to live. How can we help him? 70

25. What is the best way to prepare for death? 73

26. I'm finding it hard to move on because my parents to this date won't admit their wrongdoing and acknowledge my pain. 76

27. Is the afterlife the same experience for everybody and are there places for artists? 79

28. I keep repeating negative patterns that I can't get out of. Is my past the cause of all this negativity? 81

29. It's almost impossible for me to go back to the memories of my childhood because I can't remember anything under the age of 9. How do I reclaim my childhood memories? 84

30. Does everyone in the afterlife experience growth and evolution? 87

31. I'm a woman in my forties and my mother still disrespects my privacy. This happens to me at work too. What's going to take for things to change? 89

32. Can criminals be reformed by spiritual healing? 91

33. What do you see for the future of the planet? 94

Introduction

Since I wrote "Sacred Intentions" in 2002, I have collected questions from readers and patients that have been both personal and general in nature, questions about everyday life issues, illness, relationships, intuition, evil, God and the afterlife. It was exciting to collect such questions with the hope that I would respond to them one day. I chose thirty-three questions for this book and compiled them in a particular order which I felt would energetically transmit to the reader a flowing and developing story about the spiritual journey that we have all undertaken. Thus, I urge you to read the book as you would a novel, from beginning to end so you may feel that flow. Human curiosities tend to parallel so possibly some of the stories within these questions will resonate with your story and your search for answers.

I purposely did not answer questions about the structured and descriptive nature of the afterlife because I wanted to focus primarily on the healing opportunities and processes that exist in the afterlife. The afterlife *is* that multi-dimensional universe many authors write about, and it is *also* that place where unfinished business, unresolved affairs and unsettled feelings can find their resting conclusion as we move closer to God. I hope this book can promote further discourse on the healing processes that take place in the afterlife and how those processes can be a soulful welcome when our human journey enters the afterlife.

1

I always seem to attract relationships that are unhealthy and sometimes abusive. What do I need to change?

We can't talk about relationships without talking about healthy decision making. Making healthy decisions is one of the most important things we must learn to master in our lives. Everything we do involves decisions. We must learn to make decisions that are self-protective, self-loving, and inclusive. Happiness simply happens when we make good decisions. Who in you is making the decision to choose a certain partner or friend? Is it your heartfelt emotions, your calculated logical reasoning mind, your gut feeling and intuition, your ungrounded desires, or your fears? Let's say you walk into a doctor's office, and you are impressed by his credentials on the wall, his knowledge and his charm, but have this "bad feeling" about him. What do you do, do you walk out, or do you stay? Does it pay to stay and find out why you have this "bad feeling"? The best thing to do is to listen and trust your gut feelings and go find a doctor with whom you have "good feelings." It's all about the listening, listening to your gut feelings because that's God talking. Choose relationships by listening to your gut feelings. If you are impressed by someone but you have "bad feelings" about them, don't be influenced by your emotions. You see, emotions aren't always reliable because they can go from excitement to fear in a second. Emotions are like the ocean with many unpredictable waves. What you want is the still lake and that's what your gut feeling, intuition and instincts look like and feel like. When your emotions say yes to a relationship and your intuition says no, what do you do? You see it's possible that your emotions may dearly want someone that isn't for your highest good. Basically, our intuition is more solid than our emotions and will rarely mislead us. The guidance you get from intuition is the guidance of the still lake without the ups and downs of the ocean. On the surface, the still lake may seem boring, but underneath there is adventure, passion, and excitement.

So, you must ask yourself why am I attracting these unhealthy and uncaring relationships, what magnet in me is pulling these unhealthy folks into my orbit and most importantly what are my life lessons around intimacy? We must point the finger back at ourselves and not fall into the role of victim. If I see myself as the victim, I'll continue to attract bad relationships and fail at intimacy. The victim archetype doesn't grow and learn and therefore doesn't discover what a happy life is. So, why have you attracted these unloving and painful relationships? The answer has many layers and isn't just one simple response. I always recommend that you talk about the deeper feelings and vent so you can get to the answer. Talk with someone compassionate and wise. Dig deep into yourself to find out how valuable you are, how smart and wise you really are and what you truly deserve. Healing happens when we discover and connect to the wise person inside of us and follow the wise call and guidance.

***

2

I find myself having a very hard time forgiving myself because I feel I should be a better mother to my three kids and I'm not always a good mother.

The fact that you asked such a question and exposed such an emotional truth tells us you are a sensitive mother. One can hear the pain in your voice. The question to ask is how solid is your support system, do you ask for help and are you surrounded by loving friends and family? You can't parent if you are on empty. What is it that fills up your gas tank and inspires you? The one thing that fills us all up is love and support - love and support from your spouse, your family, your neighbors, your community, your friends. You can be a better parent when you feel filled up. When you receive from others, then you have the energy to give to your three kids from a place of patience, appreciation, and contentment. You can't expect to continue giving to the kids without getting refueled and restored. Your tank needs to be as close to full as possible for you to be a happy parent with happy children.

We celebrate Mother's Day once a year to remind ourselves that mothers need to be appreciated everyday. The gift of unconditional love that mothers demonstrate daily around the world reminds us how sacred and healing the love of a mother is. A good mother does her best to forgive herself for her mistakes and moves on to self-love because in her heart she knows she is doing the best she can do. Can she do better? Of course she can and she will all in good time. Once she secures her support system, her motherhood will be more effective and enjoyable. The joy of mothering cannot happen in a vacuum; it needs serious spousal, familial and community support. It needs teachers who care and businesses that look out for number one: the children. Now, if you are still having a hard time forgiving yourself after you have secured a support system, talk to a counselor to discover what is going on. Maybe you need to improve your relationship with yourself to discover and connect to your inner wonder, your spiritual strength, and the feeling that you are enough. Maybe you also need to evaluate your marriage and negotiate your needs with your husband. The worst thing you can do is be stuck in self-condemnation and not get help. We aren't meant to do it all alone; that belief system is deeply flawed and the cause of much misery and unhappiness. Vent to your husband or to a skilled and heartfelt counselor your hurt. An hour with a good counselor can sometimes save you months or years of confusion and struggle. We don't have to do it all alone and we were never meant to.

A good mother doesn't forget to engage in self-care. So, take care of yourself, whatever that means to you. Self-care is going to mean different things to different mothers. Self-care for you might mean opening to receive support while for another mother it might mean stopping her angry behavior and outbursts, and for another mother it might mean getting out of an abusive marriage. The greatest self-care is sitting with God in meditation and prayer for Divine Guidance. Get quiet and check in with yourself and listen to what your inner voice wants from you and for you. Does it want you to say no to negative people, yes to a better diet, exercise, and time alone, no to anger and yes to more lovemaking? Ultimately the inner voice will tell you how to be a good mother and all you have to do is listen. Self-care at its core is listening to the inner messages in order to find direction and peace. The best way a mother can engage in self-care is by tuning in, listening, honoring, trusting, and putting into action the messages from her inner voice. The Angels are talking, and we should listen.

***

3

I've been a heavy smoker since I was in my 20's and I now have lung cancer. How can I use my free will to heal myself?

Our free will can be a blessing or an impediment. As a young man, you exercised your free will to smoke and ended up with poor health. Free will gives us the authority to choose which path we want to walk. We can use it to turn right and walk into bliss or turn left and walk into a wall and I don't think there is anybody out there who hasn't said hello to a wall. How do you know which way to turn? It takes a lot of inner wisdom to know what works for you and what feels right, and that wisdom comes from listening to your inner sensors and messages. Of course, you didn't sit and consciously will yourself into a diagnosis of lung cancer. You didn't consciously invite lung cancer but it's here and you now have to process it. The good doctors will do what they can for you but that is not enough. My advice to you is process the cancer holistically. What I mean is use your free will and look at this painful diagnosis from all directions: chemical, nutritional, emotional, psychological, and of course spiritual. Pray for strength and compassion for yourself and surround yourself with people who really care about you. Go inside and pray to understand how this illness is pushing you, perhaps forcing you to change your behavior, your habits, your friends, and how it's realigning your priorities. You know how a simple cold forces us to change our plans; I'm sure this cancer is changing all your plans and all your thinking about what is important. It's forcing you to listen to what your body needs as well as what it doesn't. It isn't easy to change old ways, but you have to in order to live, if you want to live, which I know you do. Some may choose to die and get out of the body and that is their free will at work. Not everyone knows how to look at their illness holistically. It's tough to do that on a planet that promotes unawareness, non-holistic thinking, and denial. For some, death is an easier option. We mustn't judge. Our society doesn't yet have permission and isn't culturally trained to process all the sides of an illness; to do that you have to be quite modern in your thinking and step outside mainstream medicine. Medicine is not yet modern but will become modern when it starts seeing and treating patients holistically. So, let's pray that doctors in the very near future start getting trained holistically in medical schools.

Patients in the US are seen and treated in fragments, and we all know this is a very costly and ineffective enterprise in the long run. Don't do that to yourself; don't treat yourself in fragments and don't fragment your life. Your work, marriage, children, school, town, and culture are all intimately connected to your health. There is no separation; that's a big lie and an illusion. Your lung cancer is connected to speaking your truth, to feeling heard, as well as to too much smoking. You smoked all those years because it gave you some kind of comfort.

Where do you go for comfort now? Where do you go and cry out your fears and release all that grief in your lungs? Was there someone in your life that held you when you were in your twenties so your lungs would expand in full breath and joy? You see my point is that it isn't just about the cancer. There are layers here that you can access and heal if you choose to take that road. Suffering is an unwelcome teacher, so please see this illness as a window to your soul. Your soul wants you to review your unmet longings. It wants you to give yourself permission to go deep and perhaps satisfy those needs that you had to abandon and replace with cigarettes. You were filling yourself up with smoke instead of something else. What did you really want to fill yourself up with instead of smoke? Go deep and be honest. Have someone with compassion hold your hand so you can tell them the truth about what you needed and didn't get. Use your free will to exhale the pain and inhale the new possibilities. Your free will can now take you for the ride of your life as you explore your depth and discover your wholeness.

***

4

If I was a king in my last life, why do I have to work at a gas station?

Let's be clear that nothing is wrong with working in a gas station if you like it and it's a calling for you or you're doing it because you need honest money. Without my mechanic and station attendant I wouldn't be able to get around and neither would anyone with a car. So, let's be thankful to the good labor of those guys (and some ladies) with grease under their fingers. If you're having a problem working in a gas station, consider your options. If there are no other options for you currently, then please see the gas station as your teacher. What feelings have come to the surface since you started working at the gas station, shame, pride, failure, hopelessness? Please see those feelings as your window to very important life lessons. When Mrs. Jones comes to your station with her kids and asks you to fill up her gas tank and check the oil and tires, she depends on your competent and reliable service. When you were a king, thousands depended on your competent and compassionate service as well. You see life has placed you in a situation where you must serve the cars of many families whose safety depends on you. Do you see how important and powerful you are because you serve and because you are trusted? You could easily be detached and negligent and not put enough air in Mrs. Jones' front tires and watch her drive away with her kids. Her family's safety was in your power, and you chose not to care. They trusted in your power to serve, and you didn't deliver. You see, the king and the gas station attendant are both in the same line of work – service. Your royal past and your humble present are about the same life lesson: competent compassionate service that does not cast aside the welfare of others. So, when you were a king do you remember serving well? If not, here is your chance to do it again and do it right. So, you see the king and the gas station attendant have a lot more in common than you may have thought. A father is the king of his house, a professor the king of his class and you are the king of the gas station. The father, the professor and you are all needed. Your skills, your guidance and your giant hearts are needed. Being a king may keep your fingernails clean but won't guarantee to keep your heart pure and help you enter the Heavens. Look back at your life as a king and find out what legacy you left behind before your death. Did your presence make a difference for the better or did you neglect the citizenry? Death is death of the body, so the sentiments, attachment, desires, fears, hostilities, and unfinished business during one's death in a previous life carry on to the next. It appears you've carried on some unfinished business from that royal life and here you are in a gasoline station taking care of people's cars.

Your soul has brought you to this gas station for a purpose. When you start honoring and respecting this job with pride, you'll find out why you're there. This job is certainly teaching you to serve, so serve your brothers and sisters with humility and kindness because serving purifies us and purifies the soul. We travel through incarnations for three reasons: to grow mentally and emotionally (especially into humility and mercy), to have fun, and to know God. Find out how you can grow as well as how you can have fun at this gas station. See it as your sanctuary where you go to expand your heart in the service of others. When you do that, you'll feel like a king, and it won't matter that you have dirt on your pants and grease under your fingernails.

***

5

My mother died of cancer two years ago and I feel her around me especially at work. I feel that she's protecting me, but I also feel she isn't at peace with herself.

Death is death of the body. Your mother's emotional, mental, sentimental, and intellectual energy at the time of her death lives on even though her body is no longer living. If she died always feeling protective of you then she is continuing to be that way from the other side. She doesn't carry the spiritual faith that you'll be fine without her help. She doesn't have the faith that she can now turn your care over to God and move on to the Light. Her fear that you will be hurt and her lack of faith that God is looking after you keeps her around. What's important for her now is to move out of the earth plane and move into the Light. Her energy body must go to the Light for relaxation, purification, and renewal. It's best for her to go there and cleanse her energy body from the heaviness of her last life as well as the previous ones.

What tends to happen is that the earthly attachments the dead still carry keep them earthbound. It is common to find deceased parents near their living children or grandchildren. This mainly happens because of love but it delays the growth and evolution of the deceased. It's usually the love they feel that keeps them around. Your mother hasn't yet fully let go of you; are you ready to let go of her and stand on your own? If you aren't ready to do that she may not leave. When you want a helper from the spirit world always ask for one who is from the Light. A Being from the Light is free of emotional and spiritual blocks and directly in communion with God's counsel and grace. When your mother lets go of the earth plane and enters the Light, she will quickly realize how much more of a help she can be to you. The help that she is sending you now as an earthbound soul is minimal compared to the help she can send you once she enters the Light. The help that we receive from the Light is beyond comprehension; it is enormous and miraculous. Also, she needs to focus on her own healing; after all, this is a person who died of cancer and needs to seriously engage in her life review process to make things better for herself. Encourage her to move on and let her know that you don't want her help if she remains earthbound.

Can you let her go; is that an issue for you? If you're having trouble letting go of her then you'll have to look at that and dig deep for closure. Of course, the love of a mother is very very special, and it provides us great comfort. Ask God to come into your life for comfort and to send supportive and trustworthy people who are comforting to you. Since you're feeling your mother around you that tells us you have great sensitivity and intuition. Use those gifts to check in with yourself and help her to let go. Go to a sanctuary and have a talk with your mother. Light a candle and open the dialogue. Discuss with her what you want for her and what is for her highest good. Tell her that you feel she is not at peace and why that concerns you. She may initially resist your directions and advice but once she goes to the Light it will all make sense to her, and she will find peace. Her cancer and her fears will all make sense, and she will feel closure. As for the protection that you've been receiving, it's best for you and for all of us to receive help from evolved Heavenly Beings from the Light and of course from compassionate earthly beings who care about us.

***

6

Whenever I talk to my teenage daughter it seems we always end up in an argument or a fight. What can we do to get along and have more peace?

The question is what can you do to find peace in yourself? That's the proactive question we need to answer today. I'm sure you love your daughter, and it must be painful for both of you to be living with so much anger. Like a mirror, your daughter is reflecting to you something that has to do with your unhappiness and your inner anger. Are you unhappy somewhere else and your relationship with your daughter is taking the hit? No doubt she is pushing your buttons and triggering you. But what is under your anger? The more anger and yelling there are, the deeper the buried hurts. So, it's very important that you gently point the finger at yourself and do a personal review. Why is it difficult for you to stay in your softness and your heart with her and where is this impatience and volatility on your part coming from? You intuitively must know it's not all from a teenage daughter, it can't be. Something in your life outside your daughter is hurting you or has hurt you and is now turning up the anger. So how do you process that hurt?

If you find constructive and effective ways to process the hurt, or speak from the hurt instead of the anger, you will solve your conflicts with your daughter. If you quiet your mind and drop down to your softness and vulnerability, you'll feel the answers. Please let yourself go there. It's probably scary to drop down to that softness and vulnerability but that drop is what will lead you to peace. Peace with yourself first and then you will have peace with your daughter, as our energy changes so does our children's. Challenge yourself to speak from the hurt instead of the anger. Anger at times can be positive, but negative anger tends to give us this false sense that we are in control and therefore safe. It appears both you and your teenage girl are bypassing the feelings of hurt and fear and going directly to aggression because it's safer for the two of you to be in the hard emotions of aggression than the soft emotions of hurt and vulnerability. You must also look into as every parent should, how the culture outside of the home is shaping your girl. In a consumer culture like ours, it is easy for kids to be seduced into materialism, disrespect, vanity, and selfishness. Since you're the adult, it falls upon you to guide her and take the risk to speak from your softness, heart, and hurt. She must feel your heart in your words and language. Find your softness and you will find peace. As her mother please be sensitive to how your words are hurting her.

There is a golden opportunity here for you to take the relationship to higher ground. Can you feel and sense what is under her anger? It's also hurt and fear. Hurt and fear because she doesn't feel safe being in her vulnerability with you. At the core she is a softy like you, a gentle heart, and she wants you to talk to that part of her. It seems she has a warrior stance with you because she has learned it's safer to be a warrior with you than to remain a softy. So, do you have somewhere safe and soft to go to for comfort and are there adults in your life who really hear you? What keeps you in your softness? Do work, friendships and marriage keep you in your softness? If you don't have solid and consistent things in your life that keep you supported in your softness, your relationship with your daughter will probably not improve and perhaps get worse. Summon your support system, embrace your softness, and work through the hurts and fears that are under your anger; that's your solution. Pray for help and God will send you help in ways that will pleasantly surprise you. Find healthy and loving support to help you see what is beneath the anger. All that digging will eventually produce results and resolve things so you can both as mother and daughter feel your soft voices. When adults change children follow. You must change first. By doing so, you'll become your daughter's heroine and inspirational role model. So, the healing with her begins by finding peace in you.

***

7

How does long-distance healing work when someone is thousands of miles away?

Energy and intention travel thousands of miles in nanoseconds. Thought, intention, and the desire to help someone are all energy waves. The person who is receiving the healing does not have to be in the room of the healer. The waves arrive right to his aura, and he can choose to receive it or not. There is something that is important to touch on when we talk about distant healing and that is permission. Healers must first tune in and sense the green light of permission from the soul of the person they want to send a healing to. If they don't get the green light to send a healing, they should turn it over to God, let go and detach. Permission is critical or else boundaries are crossed. When there is no green light, just send good wishes and prayers to that person. Your good intentions and prayers will circulate outside the recipient's aura until he or she is ready to absorb it into their system one day, even if that's twenty years later. So, you see good intentions are never wasted, they are like money in the bank just waiting to do good. Again, don't be deceived by distance, miles, kilometers. Thought, intention, and energy transcend time and space; physics has already proved that. As we humans learn to reconnect the left and right hemispheres of the brain, we will quickly realize that the body is an expression of energy waves and patterns governed by Divine order. There is order and nothing is haphazard. It may seem things are out of order because of the suffering that is out there and the suffering within us, but there *is* order. When the mind quiets down into deep states of meditation and communion with the Divine, it will recognize order. The chattering mind can not understand Divine order or long-distance healing. Only the mind that has dropped into stillness can begin to make sense of distant healing.

If you want to know how distant healing works, quiet your mind and drop into stillness. Let the right hemisphere of your brain intimately communicate with the left. Don't take my word for it that distant healing is a possibility, be still and find out for yourself. That stillness is the greatest thing you can do for yourself, which by the way will add years to your life, good years. Healing energy that is sent to a receptive person thousands of miles away will travel and whirl before that person's aura, chakras, energy body and around the physical body. Because the healing energy has Divine intelligence, it will locate the area or areas of imbalance, deficiency, illness, and disease, and once this intelligence locates an area that needs help, it moves in to fill it with Light and therefore comfort. The person who is impatient receives the energy of patience and the person who suffers from cancer receives healing energy to increase immunity. I don't have to tell this Divine healing energy what to do when it gets to its target point. It possesses Divine Intelligence therefore it knows exactly where to go and what to do. My intention as a healer is to send the healing energy and let it serve for the highest good. My words may or may not satisfy your curiosity and intellect, but I urge you to experiment with long-distance healing yourself. Sit quietly and set an intention to help someone who is hurting, an animal, a friend, planet Earth. Send energy waves of emerald green from your hands and a ball of pink-white energy from your heart and observe without attachment to the outcome. Make sure you don't deplete yourself by giving too much and just observe. The more you do this the more you will understand how distant healing works and how its tremendous power can change our lives on this planet.

***

8

How do I know what I should pursue in college and if the career I want is for my highest good?

Make sure the career you choose contributes to your happiness and the happiness of the planet. You are young and your job is to be true to your soul's calling. For now, keep taking courses until one day soon you get a "hit" right in your heart and gut about your calling. Society asks children, "What do you want to be when you grow up?" instead we should be asking children, "What problems do you want to solve when you grow up?" If you are connected to your inner voice and your core, you will know your true wants. Deep inside you already know your true wants; they feel right, and they bring a smile to your face. Your question is about true wants versus false wants. If you are not distracted by false wants, then you'll know what is for your highest good. If you are fortunate enough to grow up in a family and a culture that does not distract you and pull you away from your core, then you'll make decisions from your core. Your core always knows what a true want is. There is a voice inside us all that tells us what a true want is if we know how to hear that voice. The voice is the voice of our core, our soul reminding us why we came here in this incarnation. The soul, the core, the inner voice, however you label it, is there to look out for us and keep us in line with our true wants and purpose.

We can't talk about children's true wants without talking about the cultures that shape them. In commercial and authoritative cultures, it is practically impossible for children and young adults to stay true to their true wants. Your family or your culture may reject your core desires and wants but be sure you don't. So do your best to not reject and betray your true wants. If you have a call to be a chef or a teacher, do that. You can probably earn a lot of money as a businessman but if that's not your calling, don't do it, if it is, go for it. Don't change your core desire for obedience, pride, or prestige, that'll ruin you and you'll become a cynic and a bitter old man. What is success for you, for *you*? Everyone must learn to define success individually. You can't know what is for your highest good if you haven't yet defined success for yourself. For your soul a successful life is a life where you take your last breath feeling that you lived from your core and contributed by helping people connect to their core, to each other and to a higher power. Ultimately, that's success and everything else is a side show. Whatever is for your highest good is also for the highest good of others. So just go out there and express that which is for your highest good and you'll make a local and maybe a global impact. Your core knows what is for your highest good so don't disconnect from your core and only surround yourself with people who respect, honor, and support your core. It's the path of false wants that has created war, pollution, selfishness, greed, and global fear and poverty. Wants that are disconnected from the soul create disconnection and separation in the world. Your question has personal, cultural, and global layers to it. To answer one layer and dismiss the others is not realistic because all the layers are intimately connected and can't be separated, not anymore. In about a hundred years we went from the industrial age to the digital, so we must think and function in global terms. We can't afford to continue pulling kids out of their core; there is too much at risk. When kids are pulled out of their core, they forget why they came here; they forget to give. So, the healing is to let your core define success for you, why? Because your core makes decisions from integrity and spiritual values. If culture and family are confusing your decisions, get quiet, go inside, and listen. What do you hear? If you live your life according to your highest good guided by your core being, then that is the greatest life you can live and the greatest contribution you can make to the planet.

***

9

Can spiritual energy healing help my children and how often would they need healing?

Spiritual energy healing can definitely help your children as long as you and your wife are involved in the process. What that means is that you as parents receive the first or maybe even the second or third healing before your children do. To work on the child without working on the parents is not wise. The energy of a child reacts and tries hard to adapt to mommy's and daddy's energy. If mommy is angry at daddy and daddy avoids mommy, then there is a triangular energetic dance at play that a child's energy must adapt to. His adaptation to this dance is going to create distortion in his aura and chakras. So, do we treat the child, or do we treat the parents? At the top of the pyramid are the grandparents, then parents, and then the children. The adults carry more history and therefore more probability for energy distortion in their auras, chakras, and energy bodies. If they have old resentments, anger, grief, or despair that they are still holding in their energy field, their sensitive children will energetically pick some of it up and react to it. So, I always recommend adults work on their personal energy healing process first before we even touch the child. Let's clear the adults of their imbalances and then work on the child; it's the easy road to healing a child and the logical thing to do.

When we work on a seventy-year-old man and shift his energy field to greater balance, the energy fields of his fifty-year old daughter and twenty-year old grandson automatically and miraculously improve; except, it's not really a miracle, it's the laws of physics at work, it's God's Divine order at work. Ancestral or generational healing for example is the healing of the emotional wounds of deceased grandparents or great-grandparents to promote healing in the living members of a family. Some children just aren't going to get better if parents are carrying old and forgotten unconscious emotional wounds. Sensitive kids energetically feel those wounds even when parents are unaware of them. Parents shouldn't blame themselves but compassionately see themselves as people who are doing their very best. When parents correct their imbalance with each other and within themselves, children improve. In most cases children improve from the treatments parents receive and at times we don't even have to work on the child.

Ideally, your children shouldn't need energy corrections once a month, but many do. The stress of school, bad teachers, peer pressure, consumerism, bad TV, and bad toys traumatize kids and take their toll. Their energy field responds to these outside stresses and becomes depleted and out of balance. The best way to reduce their need for energy healing is to make sure that we adults are tuned in to their energy and needs. By adults I also mean teachers, coaches, principals, and sitters. To heal children, you must address the adult world which directs and shapes the child world and aura. As parents, the best way we can help our kids is by being aware of our own energy supply and inner senses. The more we are aware (about children's diets too), the more we'll know why our kids get sick. When a child lives with the energy of unresolved adult conflict around him, he will be prone to a number of physical and behavioral problems. Children can't hold conflict in their bodies for too long, usually something gives. Our job as adults is to make sure we feel loved, supported, and accepted by other adults so that our energy remains whole and intact for our kids. Our children want us to be whole and intact and a spiritual family life with deep faith in God further keeps us optimistic, courageous, and magical.

***

10

Can people be possessed by evil spirits and negative energy and how can we protect ourselves?

The term possession implies we have no power or control over a negative energy. So, I want to answer your question from a healing perspective. If a person turns out to be a serial killer or a schizophrenic and cries out that he is possessed, there is a historical narrative that needs to be seriously looked at because behavior doesn't exist in a vacuum and is the result of accumulated experiences and patterns from this life and others. The term possession is too convenient and doesn't take into account a person's psychosocial and spiritual history and development. If a boy grows up with parents or a culture that is abusive and he incorporates that abusive pattern into his system by going around and abusing other kids, do we say he is possessed by an evil spirit? No, that would be irresponsible. This boy does have a mean and evil streak but look at what he witnessed growing up. So, let's not simplify a person's behavior by saying he is possessed by an evil spirit.

We can't talk about evil or negative energy without talking about fear. To talk about evil and not talk about fear completely misses and ignores the central theme and fundamental point. Basically, it is belief systems based on fear and separation that invite negative energy patterns and this is very important to keep in mind. Negative beliefs rooted in fear and separation create an opening for negative energies to enter. My experience over and over is that the negative beliefs invite negative energy and our job as healers is to not only balance the energy system but also help people replace negative beliefs with positive ones. Someone who believes that the world can't be trusted will carry a negative pattern in his aura. He will very likely have an armored shield around the solar plexus (the belly) that doesn't let people in. A healer must gently soften and remove the shield as well as discuss the concept of trust. That shield is there for good reason, so we must respect it. It helped this man survive his painful childhood. Yes, the shield is a negative energy and can produce evil, but it carries history and self-protective intelligence. So, you see it's unwise to talk about negative energies without talking about people's history and addressing the negative beliefs and the fears they harbor. The deeper question is why is evil and negativity present and what allowed the person to behave without empathy? What are the life lessons for that person carrying the negative energy? We must go beyond judging the negative energy and try to see the story behind it and eventually guide it to the Light.

The possession I like to talk about is self-possession - the individual's possession of his mental faculties, his ego strength, his emotions, his humility, and his spirituality. When people, especially children, grow up in fear and separation, it becomes impossible for them to remain self-possessed. They give up pieces of themselves to survive and end up opening the door for negative patterns to enter their energy fields. So, we must do everything we can as adults to create safety for others so that they can stay self-possessed. To protect yourself from negative energies, first and foremost remember that love without judgment is the greatest energy-force in the universe and no negative energy out there can match it. And always ask why, why is evil and that negative energy present, what lesson does it bring and what positive belief system can replace the negative one? Don't judge the negative energy; try to understand its purpose and then ask it to go to the Light.

***

11

What if a negative energy doesn't want to go to the Light?

It will go when it's ready. You can't keep pushing against a door when it doesn't want to open. If you keep pushing, you'll exhaust and hurt yourself. Leave it alone and know, really know that it's in God's hands. Everything has its season and its time. If it takes that energy a hundred years to go to the Light, we'll all have to accept that because that energy has free will. You try to overpower the will of any energy and you create backfire, that doesn't mean you don't try to open dialogue with a negative energy to guide it to the Light, but to do that, a healer must be well anchored in God consciousness. What that means is that the healer must respect the free will of the negative energy, approach it with firmness as well as compassion, and remember that higher powers are in control. Not all energies will go to the Light, but most will when their issues are resolved.

The job of a healer is to recognize the wound of the negative energy because ultimately it is the wound that prevents it from going to the Light. This is very sensitive stuff because that wound is still bleeding or else the energy would have gone to Light a long time ago. I was once asked to look over a home where a negative energy had a strong presence and sometimes materialized as a ghost that could be seen, sure enough the presence was there and so strong that I felt it ruled the land around the home. Once I tuned into the wound, what was revealed to me was that this energy refused to go to the Light because it was waiting and looking for justice. Its charge came from the emotions of rage because it felt the land was stolen from its ancestors. This energy wasn't going to leave until some kind of retribution was done; after all, its ancestors were cheated and betrayed. As a healer I had to sit with my compassion to validate the enraged feelings and let the energy feel it was being witnessed by me in a real way. I later showed it a portal of Light and directed it to that portal. I let it know that in that portal was justice and through that portal lay the deeper understanding of the laws of cause and effect and that the Light would make all the measured corrections to balance the scales of justice. At first it resisted but finally entered the portal. I may have been the first person that validated the enraged emotions of that negative energy. So the point is the wound. All negative energies or earthbound ghosts are staying around because of a wound. Some want revenge; some want pity, and some want company because they are lonely. They're all swimming in a wound of some sort and they don't know how to get out of that pool. Look for their intent and then search out the wound. The more negative, hateful, and desperate the intent, the deeper is the wound. The telepathic dialogue with these energies needs to focus on the wound in order to get results. If you focus only on their actions and negative intent, you won't resolve the problem, you'll just spiral into fear and a battle of wills with these negative energies. When they sense and feel their wound has been authentically validated and understood, they can start shifting and shedding the darkness. When you approach them with this kind of gentleness and spirituality you won't have to push them to the Light, they'll go there on their own free will. It's better to open dialogue rather than overpower the will of a negative energy. Please remember we aren't doing this work on our own, higher spiritual powers from the Light are always beside us to guide us through the process and protect us from any harm.

***

12

Do we have to come back to earth to complete our healing and learning process or can we do it on the other side?

Your spiritual guides in the afterlife will help you decide what is best for you if you care to listen. Not all of us listen. They know what is best for our healing and learning process. Your guides are really the evolved parts of you. They are your higher self that is aligned with Divine Will. Our personality will with its unenlightened self and negative ego is usually battling this higher self and its guidance. Our personality may want this or that, but it doesn't always know what is best. A lot of things can be processed on the other side but if you're supposed to learn a few things about the human journey you would have to embody a human form. Some of us have to come back to earth because we bypassed some very important lessons about being a spiritual human. Some still need to learn empathy, compassion, courage, humility and altruism and a good place for them to learn all that is on earth inside a human form. At your death if you held emotions of prejudice, rage, sorrow, despair, grief, arrogance, false pride, vanity, and other negatively charged energies and refused to go to the Light to process them, then earth is a good option for you because when you enter earth with your new body, you'll eventually have to deal with some or all of those emotions and energies. The earth experience gives us opportunities to heal and evolve in ways that are beyond measure. When you smell burning skin, see amputated limbs, hear the screams of starving children, touch the scars of war, you are transformed. The joy that we experience in the body along with the brutality we see and hear humanizes us and eventually helps us evolve. By witnessing the journey of the body, we move closer to our hearts because some of us can only move closer to our hearts if we witness the birth, the pleasures, the suffering, and the death of the body. You see the lessons learned from having a body and living with others who have a body are enormous, absolutely enormous. Ultimately, what can be learned is the spiritual law that separation is an illusion.

So, if your spiritual guides instruct you with their gentleness to go to earth, then go. It's ok to come back to earth but don't rush to come back. If you are asked to wait twenty earth years before your return, then wait. In those twenty earth years on the other side, you will heal and learn much, so you won't have to suffer here on earth. If they say twenty years don't bargain for ten and rush back to earth. Do your twenty years on the other side so your stay here on earth can be easy. Who wouldn't want an easy stay on earth, and it can be easy if you listen to the wise counsel of your higher self. Those who refuse to stay in the afterlife the suggested period of time in order to heal and grow through the wisdom of the spiritual guides and teachers, end up having a tough time on earth. Learning and growth can take place in both the physical and non-physical. The decision to process your affairs in the physical or the non-physical is going to depend on your personal history and for some of us healing is returning to earth.

***

13

What happens to us after we die?

Depends on how you die and what beliefs and emotions you take with you to the afterlife. The body dies and everything else at the time of your death remains. Everything else means your sentiments, likes and dislikes, fears and prejudices, beliefs and emotions. So, your character now as a non-physical being continues in a non-physical experience. You may not like it because you may want your body back or you may love it because you are happy to let go of your aged body. I like talking about the healing opportunities in the afterlife rather than the description of its tiers. There are many good authors and books that do a great job describing the afterlife; I like to focus on the process of transformation in the afterlife and its meaning to the overall journey of the soul. The afterlife can be what you want it to be because free will always dictates. The attachments that we form on earth and take with us to the afterlife usually shape what happens to us after we die. You can go there to gamble, to hang out and pass time, to play, to rest, to learn, or to grow, anything you choose. The afterlife can be a healing experience or an uneventful stay depending on how you exercise your free will and intentions. If your intention is to heal and become one with God, this can be a deeply meaningful and unforgettable place; so, seek Divine wealth.

Yes, it is true that we meet loved ones upon death but ultimately whether you know it or not, your deepest longing is to fuse with the energy of Light that we call God. When all the things that create separation have been shed and healed, the soul like a drop of water, slowly and gently reenters into the ocean of God. Entry into the higher tiers of Light is gradual, like a blind person who with improved vision must slowly learn to adjust to sunlight. It takes much inner work to reach those layers of evolution and wisdom where there is pure Oneness. The earth and the afterlife both offer great opportunities for evolution and growth if one cares to take advantage of them. Evolution means less and less separation from the soul and others, a process which eventually leads to the experience of bliss.

In the afterlife you do have the opportunity to heal much of what you didn't heal on earth. Let's say you die with great guilt and remorse because you didn't do right for your kids, and you take all those emotions which are energy into the afterlife. In the afterlife with the guidance of wise spiritual helpers, you can have the opportunity to transform those emotions into self-forgiveness. Not all souls that enter the afterlife utilize its holy and sacred ministry and help. Some don't like help from others, some don't feel they deserve help, some want to do it alone, some are too attached to their negative emotions, some don't see options for change, some don't trust help and some simply don't want help. Then there are those that are impatient and want to get back to earth as soon as possible, which is rarely the best option. After we die, we get an opportunity to repair, recover, grow and evolve with minimal amount of pain and suffering. Following the advice of the holy helpers who know a lot about our process is the prudent thing to do in the afterlife. They want to see nothing more than our joy. The afterlife is a place where you can shed your negative energy to open your heart to the joy within yourself and absorb more Light. All the grief, the pride, the rage, the terrors, and the hopelessness can melt away and transform. There you can also have the chance to explore your passion for the arts and visit libraries and classrooms to enrich your mind and deepen your insight and wisdom, and it's all free.

***

14

What happens to a person who commits suicide?

Some remain earthbound for several reasons, but most go to the afterlife. Those who remain earthbound eventually do go to the afterlife but in some cases will need the help of a healer to guide them back to the Light of the afterlife. When you hear about suicide, and you start digging into it with empathy and without judgment you'll be amazed at what you'll find out about yourself. You'll find out what is important to you, really important. And what is ultimately important is that our lives make sense and have meaning. When a very old man dying of terminal illness and a very young man suffering from despair both commit suicide, they arrive to the afterlife with different set of perceptions, sentiments, and emotions. For the young man life obviously didn't make much sense so death was his solution and for the old man life had completed its course and it was time to let go. When they enter the afterlife, after a very long rest, they will be asked to reflect on their final decisions on earth. In the afterlife you eventually get used to the question why. Why the illness, why the despair? You can't find solutions if the whys are ignored. Since free will dictates on earth as well as the afterlife, you don't have to deal with the whys if you don't want to, but it would be wise to do so.

There are many souls who choose to not reflect on their process in the afterlife and eagerly design their return to earth. Usually, the degree of spirituality and wisdom that one possesses before entering the afterlife can determine how much growth will take place. If the young boy opens up and decides to get help (remember free will) from the holy counsel, he will improve and anchor into hope. It's also possible that he may choose to stay in one corner of the afterlife and refuse help, which would be very sad and would prolong his pain. Help, counsel, therapy, music or art therapy, comfort, all these are available if you choose to receive them. The help offered to suicide cases is especially abundant, similar to the help offered to children who enter the afterlife. The helpers are exceptionally tender and extremely skilled in handling suicide cases. Their approach is absolutely compassionate and non-judgmental. Because they are highly evolved, they read and sense the needs and wants of the person and move the conversation (which is usually telepathic) and healing along at the person's pace. Most times they are nearby in silence, unconditional love, and stillness. They are there to listen, comfort, advise and honor the free will of the soul. Be assured that all suicide cases are immediately attended to with profound sensitivity, compassion, and comfort. Some refuse help because of intense distrust or shame but the majority welcomes it and moves forward with the healing process.

Most suicide cases are urged to not return to earth until their healing process is completed. Their healing has a lot to do with rebuilding their energy container which acts as a shield protecting their boundary from the intrusion of negative thoughts and emotions. They get to learn why the container that once protected them from suicidal thoughts broke down. In the healing process they get to ask all the whys about themselves and get them answered gently and with patience. Their mental and emotional fields are rebuilt and strengthened during the healing process to help them reconnect to their passions and soul mission and purpose. Many who recover choose to train in becoming helpers and stay in the afterlife while those who return to earth tend to get involved in the helping professions and spirituality. Their outcome in the afterlife is usually very promising when help is received. Because of their intense need for direction and guidance most accept the help and unconditional love offered in the afterlife and become true seekers of truth and Light.

***

15

How do you define what a spiritual life is?

Anything that creates separation between people cannot be spiritual or produce long lasting love. The highest degree of spirituality is experiencing separation as an illusion. Any experience that highlights and focuses on the differences between people creates separation. If I emphasize my religion with an air of superiority, I create separation and commit an unspiritual act. Being religious doesn't mean a person is living a spiritual life. The holy of holies and the sacred don't focus on your religion and race because the holy and the sacred don't emphasize and stress differences. We may look at ourselves and claim we belong to this religion or that, to one sect or another, but to Heaven we belong only to one real thing – Divine Love. As humans, it is important for us to feel belonging because it gives us a sense of comfort, identity, and continuity but ultimately what we belong to is Divine Love.

A strong expression of a spiritual life is the courage to dissolve separation between people. The spiritual journey pleads with us to focus on the similarities between us and not promote separation. At the core we all need and want the same thing - a life that is heartfelt, safe, meaningful, and one that gives us the opportunity to grow and move closer to God. A spiritual life is a concern for others, living by the Golden Rule, and sensing that the other is connected to me. When a person isn't connected to his humility and his heart, it becomes easy to see others as separate, as something to exploit and control. If I'm separated from my heart, it's easy to justify why someone's color, race and religion are inferior to mine. The most important spiritual act any of us can engage in is to try to reconnect to our sacred inner stillness and create an environment for others to do the same. The sacred that's inside each one of us knows there is no separation because it lives in the heart and has transcended race, color, tribe, and religion. When a Chinese boy is raised with love and respect by an African family, will that boy feel intolerance to dark skin? No, he only feels love because love was what was given to him. He has transcended color barriers and can see and feel the soul of his dark skin neighbors. I guess you can define spirituality as the ability to feel and see the soul of another person, not just your kid's and your tribe's. Very evolved spiritual beings can feel and see the Light of even the cruelest of human beings because they have the ability to recognize that cruelty is a front for deeply buried wounds.

The question about what is really spiritual comes down to how well you are connected to your inner Light. When you and I are connected, really connected to our Divine Light, it becomes very easy to see the human being in front of you as Divine Light and separation basically dissolves. You start treating him as you would treat a brother you care about. If you're a soulful land developer, you won't exploit the land because the land is your mother, and you won't construct poor buildings because you know your brothers and sisters are going to live in them. Connection to your soulful song is spirituality and opening up to soulful action and service helps maintain a spiritual life. Dictators and criminals live in separation because they are separated from their Light and their soulful song. Their song was silenced years ago and they're so angry about it that they're going to silence everybody else's. Pray that they remember their song. The more you and I do our best to dissolve separation in ourselves, the better the outlook for all and for the planet. Our valiant efforts to live spiritually today will help keep future generations anchored in their hearts and spiritual purpose tomorrow. It's funny how one candle can spread light to a dark giant cave; you and I can be that illuminated candle.

***

16

Are some children born with more spirituality than others?

You often hear people say that someone is an old soul. A small clarification - an old soul doesn't mean an evolved soul. Someone could have had many lives on earth without experiencing profound inner and spiritual growth. By evolved we mean "they are their brother's keeper." The more evolved a person the less he or she sees separation between people. Many of the souls coming to earth since the 1970s are highly evolved and are what some call the Indigos because their aura about the head consistently shows that color. Since the mid 1990s, there has been another group coming in with platinum-silver color auras about their heads. These souls along with the Indigos will be involved in the spiritual evolution and uplifting of the planet. As the decades roll on, more and more evolved babies will enter the planet to promote greater spiritual planetary growth. Together, these souls will be and some already are the future movers and shakers and in less than two hundred years from now they will run the show and Amen to that. They are spiritual because they operate in the "We" consciousness; they always think about what's in it for us and not only what's in it for me. Their interest in the accumulation of wealth and power is for the sole purpose of service to others. Souls like these are mostly from the Celestial sphere and their mission is to elevate the human consciousness to higher spiritual planes and Divine Love. They've chosen to incarnate at a crucial time in history when they will be most needed by the masses. They think and live globally, and most are masters of the global technologies that are at their fingertips. They are wizards on the computer, and they use it to generate connections with other kids on the other side of the globe. They also know how to have clean fun. In the afterlife they had paid attention and attended all the necessary classes to clear their issues and ground into their mission on earth. Some have come with memories, and they can tell you what the other side looks like and what former lives they have lived. More spiritual here means more connection to one's Divine identity and memory of that identity.

These evolved kids don't draw their core identities from race, culture, religion, and country; they are beyond those definitions and draw their identity mainly from their spiritual values and divinity. Because they came here to earth with great purity of heart, they carry inside them a strong moral code and a sense of deep justice. In the afterlife, they attended educational centers that offer courses and classes in diplomacy, psychology, meditation, mediation, law, art and literature, philosophy, ethics, theology, and of course love; yes, classes about how to express and spread love in the universe. Not all souls show an interest or care to attend such courses but those who do become the souls that shift global thinking and action here on earth. So, the spiritual quality of a new incarnate is dependent on three things: his ability to remember Home - God, his accumulated wisdom from the afterlife lessons, and his growth and development from past incarnations. When a baby enters the earth with these three ingredients, the earth is blessed with wisdom and power. Power because when a soul walks the earth with a giant heart anchored in spiritual teachings, darkness just steps aside. Darkness is no match to the light of this baby. Time is always on the side of spirituality because evil is always running out of time and options. By its nature evil is always on a course of self-destruct, always. It's just a matter of time before evil disintegrates. And when more and more spiritual children incarnate in the coming decades, negativity will recycle to Light.

***

17

When I'm trying to decide something important how do I know I'm making the right decision?

You'll know when your heart, your head and your gut feelings agree with each other. If you aren't sure about a decision, be patient and wait, in a few hours or days or months it'll become clear. When you can't be objective about your life decisions because your emotions come into play, get someone objective and wise to help you. Trust your gut feelings in decision making. Don't rule it out or throw it away, second guess it or overanalyze it. Our gut feeling is a powerhouse that we all need to trust and respect. If you stay calm and turn down the volume of fear and excess desire, you'll hear your gut feeling clearly. Gut feeling is an inner knowing that we are all born with and the voice of our higher self and God. When fear or excess desire rule your emotions, it's very hard to hear and sense your gut feelings. Fear keeps you ungrounded and, in your head, and an overexcited desire can keep you in your swaying emotions. Nothing is wrong with desires as long as they're for your highest good but as we all know not all desires are for our highest good. Some desires will get you lost. Living in a global culture of commercialism makes it very easy to get lost in wrong desires. Don't go only with your head or your heart; bring in your gut feeling in the decision making. Your good heart may want to give and give to a neighbor until one day you realize that all that giving didn't change a thing. If you had listened to your inner knowing you would have known giving to that neighbor was a mistake. Nothing is wrong with giving but let your inner knowing direct your giving.

The two big mistakes most people usually make about decisions are distrust of their intuition and not getting the advice they need. You don't have to make decisions by yourself. There are a lot of healthy, competent, and compassionate people out there that can answer most of your tough questions. In the age of the internet, it is easy to find supportive communities near where you live. We don't have to do it alone and we were never meant to. Patience is another important ingredient in decision making. Sometimes you don't know if you're making the right decision and that is why you should wait, meditate, get quiet, get help and be patient. If you're unsure about an important life decision, don't be pushed into it if you aren't ready to make the necessary commitment. It takes courage to say no to others and yes to yourself and inner knowing. Ultimately, the things that make you feel alive and produce good warm feelings are the things that are good for you. Ask your body about a decision and sit back and observe what you sense in your body. Learn to be a witness to your body's senses and responses without judgment. Does your body contract, does your breathing change, are you feeling peace? Let go the attachments you have to an outcome and observe. Get very very familiar with how your body reacts to decisions. Your body will know if a move, a new job, a new friend, a new relationship, or a new car is the right thing for you. God and the Angels send signals and messages through your body if you can be still and listen. Turn down the noise in your head, be still with your emotions, and bring your focus down into your body to get the answers. It takes practice to get good at this but it's the most important thing you can do for a better life because a good life, a happy life, is a result and a product of good decisions.

***

18

Does prayer work and can God give me what I pray for?

Prayer does work but what if what you're praying for is not for your highest good? So be careful what you pray for. Prayer is an energy that is governed by spiritual laws and those laws direct actions in certain ways. The most important spiritual law about prayer is asking for that which is for your highest good. Prayer is the act of asking from God. Before you ask for something check if it is aligned with God's plan, which is your soul's plan. You may ask for a promotion and later discover that promotion becomes a curse and gives you an ulcer. Be careful what you ask for, what you pray for and where your intentions lie. Let your asking be aligned with your soul's will. Let the soulful place in you ask, not the personality in you that has flaws. Our soul knows best what we need, and the right thing to do is to be in touch and in full contact with the soul's voice and guidance. You do that by getting quiet, dropping inside, and listening. So, before you ask, listen to your soul. Your intention to have this outcome or that thing is hopefully a soulful one. Wants and desires define who we are and ignite our life force and that's a good thing. The objective is to have an intention that works for us instead of an intention that makes us sick. Intentions can go either way. It always works best when they are aligned with the wants, desires, and longings of the soul. You'll know which intention is aligned with your soul if you listen and trust your gut knowing. If you want and desire a cottage in the country and if that want and desire is aligned with your soul, God will help you get it. If your want and desire for that cottage is not aligned with your soul, you may get your cottage but you're not going to be a happy camper. If you're praying for a loved one who is sick remember to honor their free will and God's plan. This gets a little tricky if you don't understand and appreciate spiritual laws. You may want your mom or your best friend to get well but if their journey calls for sickness, you'll have to learn to surrender to that. The highest prayer you can offer for others is for them to align with their soul purpose. When people are aligned with their soul purpose their life moves along with minimal conflict and illness.

God honors our free will and is always ready to help, so pray wisely and be wise about your prayers. Getting what you pray for isn't always going to make you happy if your soul's direction and purpose lie elsewhere. So how do we know what to pray for? If you are confused about what to pray for, pray for balance and pray to connect with the wisdom of God's plan within you. When that happens, your life is without contradiction and is in full balance. God is balance. The Celestial energies are not in conflict because they are in balance. It's like a family who adopts a child and automatically feels balance, or a young woman whose new job brings to her balance and makes her feel complete. The energies of the darker spheres of the afterlife are dark because they are in search of balance.

Pray to feel balanced, complete, whole, holy. Pray to have balanced emotions and a balanced mind. Healers are always balancing the energies of their patients: yin-yang, feminine-masculine, doing-being, assertion-tenderness, work-play, the list goes on. Anyone who is balancing energies and the scales of justice is serving God and God's prayer is that we pray for and move toward balance. Each one of us is a drop of the ocean called God and therefore we are co-creators. If you pray for something that is for your highest good, you will create joy and if you are praying for something that doesn't serve your soul you will create conflict and imbalance.

***

19

What is the afterlife like?

Just like earth the afterlife has many colors, shapes, and places. If you practice getting quiet and dropping into your core, you'll start remembering what the afterlife is like. Suffering is the inability to remember who we are and where we came from. The world is full of distractions that promote forgetting so go to nature and let it be your vehicle for remembering. The afterlife is non-physical layers of energy spheres where we go after our physical death. The different layers carry different energy waves to accommodate different emotions and mental energies and thoughts. There are entry points for those who have just died. There are different entry points depending on one's death. Someone dying from a shotgun blast will go to an entry point that is very different than someone who died a peaceful death. It helps a lot, a great great deal, to have faith in a higher Divine power. If you believe life ends at the point of physical death, your energy body will hover in confusion and loss until one day you decide to communicate with your spiritual guides and helpers. At the entry points we are met by loved ones who are eager to greet us and by our spiritual helpers who are usually more evolved than ourselves. After connecting with our loved ones, we are advised by our guides. The advice and counsel have to do with moving us to higher understanding and to the processing of the negative beliefs and unfinished emotions of the earth life or lives. The guides will instruct you where to go for higher learning, healing, growth, and evolution. In our life review process, they help us make sense of the purpose of our good and as well as bad earthly experiences and assist in plotting future courses for our soul development. If we follow the guidance of our gentle guides and the counsel of our life review Angels, we can quickly move to higher frequency layers and learn the truths we have always been searching for.

To a large extent the afterlife is similar to the earth experience with places that vibrate at low as well as high frequencies. Free will dictates, so if you want to go to low frequency layers where you can indulge in negative pleasures such as gambling and gossiping you have the free will to do that, of course it's not advisable. In the higher frequency layers, you can learn languages, music, art, and everything imaginable. The afterlife, like earth, provides opportunities for instruction and positive pleasures. There are libraries, conservatories, music halls, art galleries, hospitals, monasteries, cities, and landscapes, holographic duplicates of what we know here. Your sensory experience of all this is not like that of earth; here you sense with your energy body and communication is telepathic, your energy body with its thought and heart consciousness experiences the stimuli. Because it is easy to get distracted by visiting the many interesting locations that exist in the afterlife, it's best to follow the directions given to you by your guides. Let them help you navigate through the different layers because they know what is best for you. You could say the afterlife is a continuation of the earth plane - a place where you can learn a career, master certain emotional qualities, meet other souls, and gain better understanding of the higher Celestial sphere. It is designed for the purpose of growth and connection with others on a soul level if you choose to take advantage of it. Think of the layers as classrooms with different grades offering thousands of courses, each course opening the door to a more exciting adventure. Just like earth, the afterlife is a place that offers adventures in learning and advancement. In the higher frequencies of the afterlife, you begin to dissolve the individuated "I" and connect to the "We" and the Oneness. It is here where we commune with highly evolved spiritual beings emanating Light.

***

20

How can we get in touch with our intuitive side?

Through silence as well as activity. Certain activities connect people to their intuition: dancing, singing, walking, cooking, riding a bike, music, gardening, yoga, martial arts, playing cards, the list goes on. Intuition doesn't only come in through silence and meditation. So, what is the activity for you? Find it and stick with it as often as you can. I have a patient whose intuition kicks in when she is running and another patient who hears her inner guidance when she is cleaning. Silence as well as the "sacred activity" that works for you will help you hear yourself. When we silence the chattering mind in a sacred and quiet location or through your favorite "sacred activity," the intuitive side within us drops in effortlessly and gives us the answers and guidance. We can't hear our soul in the midst of chatter, and neither can our kids. Children especially need silence to hear and feel themselves and remain connected to their intuition. A great deal of healing takes place when people drop into their 'sacred silence and activity' to connect to their soul's guidance. It is important to get in touch with our intuition so we can make better decisions. We create happiness by making good decisions. Intuition is our soul talking to us and it is God's link to our human existence. Intuition is the voice of our soul trying to guide our actions and thoughts into good decision-making. It is the gut knowing and we need to trust that knowing. Intuition helps balance the decisions that come from our heads and hearts. If we made decisions and lived only from our heads and hearts without our intuitive gut feeling and knowing, we wouldn't be very happy; we would remain disconnected from soulful living and we would be ruled by logic and swaying emotions. When intuition is balanced with sound reason, it can be a trustworthy pilot and a guide we can rely on in difficult times. For many people it's very difficult to do all this that we're talking about. We all have the ability, but we don't allow ourselves to practice it perhaps because we fear it or because the modern culture we live in promotes over-thinking, over-stimulation and constant distraction. Kids are losing their soul connection because of excessive screen time and social media. Additionally, when you go through the educational systems of western societies that are strongly reason based with little if any study of nature and human intuition, you come out somewhat disconnected from your core and your intuition.

Find silence and connect to a community of people who are interested in spiritual development. In that silence try to silence the chatter of the mind and just be a witness to whatever happens. Learn to meditate. Watch your breath in and out. Meditation is the act of non-doing and non-thinking and it is in this state that you receive guidance and inspiration. Try to reduce over-thinking and just be for a few minutes a day. Be present to yourself without self-judgment and fear and know that God is your partner. Also, please let yourself experience nature as a cathedral.

Nature is our link to the Divine. Spend as much time as you can in places and locations that are clean, peaceful, and quiet. A walk in the woods, a stroll by the ocean or a climb to the mountain all bring us closer to our core and intuition. Make nature a part of your daily life and introduce it to your children in a big way. Mass media culture that children consume in large doses pulls them away from their center and core in ways we can't yet imagine. It is the responsibility of adults to protect children from invading commercial forces that are all around them. Introduce them to nature, to spiritual values, to charity and altruism so they can stay connected to their intuition and to who they are. In one corner of your home create an altar and go there daily in silence with your little ones to reconnect to the larger parts of you anchored in the sacred, love, and wisdom. Make your home and nature the places that inspire you and keep you in touch with your intuitive side.

***

21

I am married to someone who refuses to be accountable and tries to always convince me that I'm the one who needs to change. He won't go to counseling with me and after twelve years I don't know what my next move should be.

Please be honest and ask yourself what it is you're supposed to learn from this conflict of twelve years. When you answer that question your twelve years will have meaning. When you look at your marriage as an evolutionary process, how have you evolved? You may need the help of a professional to answer this question and process your emotions and beliefs about it. So, what are the lessons you are supposed to learn from all this? You have a number of choices, and your best choice is to continue to grow even if he refuses to. Make it about yourself, your growth, and focus less on what he doesn't do. There is a possibility that your partner may not change or learn to be accountable in this life. Please pray for the courage to grow and the strength to accept the possibility that he may not change. What you are discovering and learning is that you deserve and want to be with someone who is accountable. You are becoming more connected to healthy wants and needs and to your greater sense of deserve. This is all good and shows how you have evolved, that you are no longer tolerant of immaturity. Ask yourself, why was I so tolerant of the past? Don't stop your evolution. Continue to ask questions and find the answers and you will find the answers because your soul wants you to find the answers. When you're honestly searching for happiness, God and your Angels will open the doors. If you keep looking to change, you'll move to a better life. The first thing you have got to do is create a support system. That means compassionate, non-judgmental, and wise family members, friends, or therapists. No room for negativity, pessimism, and judgment. You tolerated unaccountability for twelve years and now you are preparing to close that chapter. That means you are no longer willing to tolerate people who are unaccountable, including your husband. Pray for strength and for growth, but also pray for his growth. Your prayer for him is like money in the bank which his energy will use on a rainy day.

All unaccountable people, all, eventually face their humbling hour because that is how spiritual laws play out. It's not a punishment but rather an energy balancing that happens when folks resist growth through self-examination. The energies are always looking to balance, so when we refuse to balance and grow through self-examination, we are forced to balance and grow through crisis. We can't stop growth because the soul is always looking for expansion, growth, and union with God. The more rigidly we resist growth, the more chaos we will attract. We can grow through gentle self-examination or through pain. Growth can't be stopped because we are beings in the moving wheel of evolution towards God.

And because you are now looking for a partnership that demands accountability, you have moved to a new level of growth which means you will now attract people who are accountable. Don't get lost focusing on your husband to change; that may or may not happen. The focus should be on your changes. Pray for and work on self-love and strength. When your degree of self-love increases you will no longer want to be with people who don't value you and refuse to be accountable. Your greater self-love will increase your self-worth and you will discover how valuable you are and how valuable your time is. It takes strength and courage to make the changes that you're considering so make sure you have a reliable support system. Please remember we were never meant to take on the challenges of change all alone and by ourselves, so reach out both for spiritual and human sources for help.

***

22

What is the best way to control and stop evil?

By reducing fear. Most people, including professionals, think that hate and rage is what feeds evil. They define evil through the language of aggression. They're mistaken because what feeds evil is fear. Under hate, rage, violence, and brutality is the fear and terror of opening the heart. The opposite of love is not hatred but fear and the lack of faith in God. The question becomes what closed the heart of the criminal and what experiences erected his walls of separation from others. However you dissect evil the conclusion is always fear, but you got to look deep to find it. Evil is a defense and a compensation to a wounded heart. If you honestly review (which is rarely done) the life of a dictator or a hardened criminal, you'll find fear and terror hiding underneath all the brutal acts - fear and terror of connecting to others and needing others. This fear didn't happen in a vacuum; families, educators and cultures consciously or unconsciously contributed to it. If we want to stop evil, we must learn to reduce fear and create safety. If we don't reduce fear, we won't reduce evil. Of course, not all individuals who grow up with fear and terror become evil. Some become lawyers who fight for justice or politicians who advocate humane policies. The act of evil committed by a person, a group or a race is so shocking to most of us that we find it hard to believe the perpetrators are acting out their fears. Does an evil person have the capacity to feel your emotion of fear and vulnerability, and can he empathize? Well, there was a time when the evil person as a young child could feel empathy and vulnerability and could feel his heart and yours. There was that time, but it's long gone. What happened, what closed the heart? Hellish events happened for sure. A brutal and painful childhood happened that left no room for tenderness and sweetness.

We can't talk about evil without talking about preventing brutal and painful childhoods because it is brutal and painful childhoods that give rise to evil. So, if you know your neighbor is beating up on the kids and your mayor is discriminating against "those people," make some noise because God wouldn't want you to sit there and be quiet. You must understand that for the evil person it is less scary to brutalize someone than to open the heart. Again, what closed the heart? That's the question to ask whenever we're dealing with evil because something, someone or some horror closed that heart. It is shocking and profoundly disappointing that mental health professionals at the top of their field don't to this day discuss the subject of evil in a comprehensive and clear way. They tend to focus on the aggressive psychology of evil and dismiss the reality and history of fear which is always and always the common denominator in the childhoods of murderers and dictators. The fear is so deeply buried that most people don't even think, sense, or believe that it exists. You can't describe and define evil without talking about fear. Biographers of dictators and serial killers need to write as many pages on the genesis of evil as they do on the horrific descriptions of evil acts. Evil doesn't just spring up from nowhere, it develops. So, we stop evil by being honest about how evil grows and develops. Let's have forums, conventions, and conversations about how evil develops because it is spiritually, emotionally, culturally, and economically very costly to not do so. When we come across or learn about someone who is evil, we must do all we can to protect ourselves from the evil in that person, but we must also remember the Divine spark of goodness that resides dormant and buried in that same person under layers and layers of fear and terror.

***

23

Do I need to belong to a religion to live a spiritual life?

A knife can cut a ripe fruit or cut down human life. If you carry darkness in your heart, your religion will become a weapon and not a sacred voice. Religion isn't going to make you a spiritual person if you refuse to clear out your bitterness, intolerance, false pride, and rage. You'll get out of religion what you bring and put into it. If you wrap yourself around a religion and still want to hold on to your racism and sexism, you won't know what a spiritual life is. A spiritual life is an ongoing daily process of shedding separation from God and others. History shows over and over that a religious life doesn't necessarily mean a spiritual life. Your life can be spiritual with or without religion. If you raise a child without religion but with lots of tenderness, encouragement, acceptance, and guidance, he will know God, but he will call it love. Love is God and God is love. A spiritual life is a life where love makes most of the decisions. The more decisions you make from love the more spiritual energy you possess. Spirituality is the recognition that we are one and the actions we take to become one. Lack of spirituality is the fostering of disconnection with one's divinity and seeing others as separate from you. It's good if your experience of your religion connects you to others and helps you see others as your brother and sister beyond their religion, race, tribe, color, gender, and heritage. If going for a walk in the woods keeps you connected to

God, then those woods are your path to spirituality and are your religion. And if the smiles of children keep your neighbor connected to God, then the children are your neighbor's path to a spiritual life. God doesn't care if your connection to a spiritual life happens through nature, children, or religion.

Whatever keeps your heart open and connected to the higher powers is your path to spirituality. It could be the woods, children, prayer, rocks, your horse, the sky, thunder, rain, sunshine. If you think everyone in the world should follow the teachings of your religion, you're being controlling, judgmental and divisive and therefore non-spiritual. When religion moves into the territory of mine and yours, it's no longer spiritual. When a religious leader speaks up for the rights of his flock and stays quiet about violations against another religious flock, he isn't being a spiritual leader. Spirituality doesn't take a rest because your neighbor has a different color, language, and race. Unfortunately, most religious leaders are tribal in nature and rarely help or defend groups from another religion. Religion teaches us that we are our "brother's keeper" but when religious leaders worship God on religious holy days but fail to speak up and protect their flock from political, social, and economic injustice, are they being spiritual? So, anything that keeps you in your heart will lead you to a spiritual life. Children and nature are the greatest inspiration and source of wonder in our lives. Children keep us in our hearts and nature keeps us guessing about the great mysteries of the universe. Before there was religion, people's connection to God came through nature. If you live a life that honors children and respects nature, your life already has a strong spiritual quality, and you are closer to God than you think.

***

<u>24</u>

My father is in his 80's and very sick for over a year. He is near death but has a strong will and fights everyday to live. How can we help him?

Through prayer. Pray that he opens up to the non-physical world of the afterlife and gives himself the chance to go there. Sleep will help. Let him sleep as much as he can. Sleep will give him the opportunity to leave the body and visit the non-physical reality. Sleep is a good way to slowly detach from the earth plane and become acquainted and familiar with the afterlife. His visits there during sleep will help him let go of his physical body with less fear. When someone in his situation is fighting death, there are usually a number of underlying reasons. The four most common reasons are worth mentioning. Top of the list is lack of faith and a poor understanding of God and the afterlife. The better someone understands the nature of spirituality, the easier the journey of dying. In the future we will have more evolved spiritual leaders whose teachings about death and the afterlife will be clearer and more comprehensive. Their teachings will better prepare those who are dying and reduce the fear of death. A second reason is the unmet longings and unlived dreams; the pains of could've, should've, would've. This issue is an umbrella of unresolved and unfulfilled emotions and fantasies. "I should've talked to my kids; I could've moved to Colorado, I would've opened that business if only..." Many who die have unfinished emotional pains and conflicts and don't always understand that this unfinished business can be attended to in the afterlife. They feel they are dying with the unmet dreams and longings and therefore feel trapped by their grief. They don't want to die because they are still holding on to those regrets and longings and are unable to let them go. In the afterlife, extremely compassionate, wise, and skilled counselors and guides are available to attend to every loss imaginable. No matter how much darkness one brings to the afterlife, the afterlife can provide Light, vision, direction, and strength for those who ask for help.

The third reason this fight with death goes on is because of the need for forgiveness. It's an emotional issue like the second but for me as a healer it is in a category of its own because of its intense energy charge and consequences. It's a sad thing to witness people who can't forgive others or themselves at the time of death. The inability to forgive freezes and shuts down the possibilities for growth and transformation and stops the healthy emotions from coming in. The dying person becomes a prisoner to this freeze and the process of death turns to a battle. It is crucial that dying people are safely encouraged to speak about matters that deal with forgiveness and self-forgiveness. Speaking will help them soften and let go of their battle. Those who open up and go through the process of forgiveness embrace death more easily and die with peace. If they go to the afterlife with unresolved feelings of forgiveness, they will continue the battle until they decide to ask for help. So, pray that your loved ones learn to be receptive to spiritual help once they enter the afterlife. Your prayers are a tremendous help. The fourth reason has to do with attachments - attachment to people, things, and to the human senses and appetites of the body. Separating from family, children, good friends and loved ones leaves behind emptiness and makes it very difficult for us humans to depart from earth. The healing that takes place in the afterlife fills the empty heart with joy and teaches souls that death doesn't mean separation from loved ones. To summarize, the major reasons why people fight death are: lack of faith, grief of unmet longings and dreams, forgiveness issues, and attachments to people, things and to the senses and appetites of the body. There is an entire army of Angelic Beings in the afterlife eagerly prepared to help us overcome our fears and attachments and facilitate our transition from physical death to spiritual rebirth.

***

25

What is the best way to prepare for death?

When some people find out they are at death's door, they begin to make arrangements. They begin to forgive, let go of bitterness, make amends, speak from the heart and higher self, and try to bring things to closure. They begin to say, 'I love you' and 'I'm sorry' and so their death turns out to be a good death. The face of a person who has had a good death looks serene and peaceful. To prepare for a good death one must try to live a good life. Those who know why they came to earth and live out their purpose die well because they die fulfilled. Those who get lost somewhere in the corridors of life and seductive cultural forces don't live out their purpose and generally fear death. So, remain optimistic and live out your purpose and don't worry about death. See God as your partner in all your endeavors and you'll create a good life and when death knocks on the door you'll open it without fear. Those who live their purpose welcome and embrace death when the time comes. If you make your life about authentic service to others, you will have authentic human attachments and your death will be clean. What I mean here is the more real you are the better you are prepared for death and serving others makes us real. Serving pushes us outside of our self-absorption and helps dissolve separation from others.

Serve and know God as your partner and death will feel like a swim in new adventurous waters. Make it your job to learn about giving and master the art of giving because giving will prepare you for a good death. Give when you can what you can without burning yourself out. Make giving your primary expression. Give with humility and without false pride. Giving will give you meaning to live and when you have lived with meaning your life is complete; your candle burns to the bottom and gently goes out. When your life has deep meaning and substance, death is no longer a scary thing because you have lived a full life. You can't be prepared for death if you fear it and the fear is usually a result of an unfulfilled life. So, what fulfills you and what is it that gives you meaning and purpose? Search hard and find the things that will fill you up.

It's good to want to see the world, have a nice set of clothes, eat wonderful meals, and build a family and an amazing career. Those are great things we all deserve, but once we've secured our comfort we must learn to extend and stretch ourselves in the care and welfare of the less privileged. If it's always about you, you'll never have enough, and when you don't feel you've had enough, you'll never be ready for death. It's a transcendent experience to hear someone say, 'I've lived enough.' It takes wisdom and stillness to develop a friendly and peaceful relationship with death because it takes a lifetime to teach the self-absorbed self to extend its heart beyond itself. So, sit down and have a chat with death in full honesty. Tell death all about your fears and what you like and dislike about it. Ask it to teach you how to get ready for your departure from earth. But don't think too much about death; think more about living and giving. Think about making this life enough. But our lives can never be enough if we don't make an effort to contribute to something, something worthwhile – saving a whale, reducing pollution, teaching an old man to read, stopping corruption. Go out and find your calling and contribute. Be a father and a mother to something that moves you and makes your heart sing. When we contribute, we feel enough, and when we feel enough we accept death's calling with grace. Our contribution serves two enormous functions – it prepares us for a good death and leaves behind a better planet, and that will just feel magical and enough.

***

26

I'm finding it hard to move on because my parents to this date won't admit their wrongdoing and acknowledge my pain.

Let's focus on your life lesson. First know that the healing process of your parents is in God's hands, and you can help by your prayers for them. Pray that they develop the strength to become accountable and responsible. You don't feel that your negative experience with them has been validated and that's a painful thing. Go to that pain with the help of a therapist and bring it to a conclusion. Let someone witness your pain about all this - the pain of not being heard, not being acknowledged, not being counted. Let a compassionate and non-judgmental human being witness all the emotional layers of your story. There is rage, sorrow, hurt and fear. Ask God for help and go through the different layers however long it takes. Once you are done, you'll find it easy to let go of this story and forgive your parents. Don't expect your parents to change because they may not. Your healing comes when you go into your process of grieving the loss of your ideal relationship with your parents and the loss of your innocence. Don't make this about them, make it about your process of shedding layers of emotion and grief. You have an amazing story and an opportunity that is pushing you to feel. Don't judge feelings, just feel them because they are all real and they'll make you more real. They'll make you whole. If you sit in blame and self-pity your energy system will never be whole.

From a spiritual perspective your soul is connected to your parents and the three of you chose to incarnate at this time to balance your energies. Since free will dictates, we all have something to do with the choice of our parents whether we believe it or not. When you sit in silence and in meditation your memory will open up. You'll begin to remember the experience of "choice" before your arrival to earth. Your energy system (made up of beliefs, emotions, thoughts, and memories) attracted these two parents because your energy system needed something from them in order to balance itself. Your pain, because of their lack of accountability, is pushing your system to drop into grief and deep emotion. When you drop into the grief and deep emotion and come out on the other side, you'll balance your energy system and on your next journey to earth you'll choose parents who are more evolved and healthier. When your energy system is balanced things will start making sense. We're all here on earth balancing our energy system. If your energy system can't easily feel or express frustration, it will attract other energy systems that will trigger and bring to surface your frustration. You as an energy system needed to feel certain feelings and learn about the importance of accountability and you chose to do it with this set of parents. Energy systems are always looking to be whole and when they aren't whole, they'll search and find outside energy systems to push them to wholeness. We attract energies that are missing in us or out of balance within us so we can become whole. The passive person will attract the aggressive in order to learn self-defense and aggression. The arrogant person will attract the energy of illness, humiliation, or loss in order to learn humility. Our energy system is always looking to be whole and if we can't or refuse to search and find our missing pieces then outside energies will come in to do it for us. One day in this life, in the afterlife, or in the next incarnation, your parents will attract energies that will burst open their hearts and teach them empathy. Give yourself the gift of balancing your energy and God will look after the energy system of your parents.

***

27

Is the afterlife the same experience for everybody and are there places for artists?

No, it isn't the same experience for everyone. The afterlife becomes what you bring to it and how flexible you are to receiving divine instructions and guidance. It helps to be a good listener and humble enough to admit that you don't have all the answers and that you don't know it all. Humility goes a long way in the afterlife as well as the earth life, but if one remains inflexible, prideful, arrogant, and egotistical in the afterlife, they can exercise that option. So, the afterlife for a humble person is going to be a whole lot easier than for an arrogant one. The help and support given to a humble soul is going to be in the mega-doses compared to a soul who doesn't want help or doesn't think he needs it. The angelic realm is completely ready, willing, and able to elevate the consciousness of any soul that will ask and receive. What you experience in the afterlife is whatever emotions, beliefs, and sentiments you bring to it. If you go to your death a staunch racist, you will be approached by the Divine to consider the teachings of tolerance and brotherhood. You have the option to refuse those teachings and stay a racist since free will dictates and thus your existence in the afterlife will probably be among other racists who advocate your beliefs and sentiments. You will attract those in the afterlife who vibrate and resonate with your emotions, thoughts, and beliefs. The corrupt politician will be among other corrupt politicians, the ruthless CEO will be among his ruthless peers, the sexist will hang out with sexists and the bigot will hang out with bigots. The afterlife accommodates all, and energies of the same kind tend to stay together just like they do on earth. For those who want to and love to grow emotionally and spiritually, the afterlife experience can be extremely exhilarating and rewarding, but for an impatient soul who is eager to get back to earth the afterlife can feel like a prison.

Assistance and help are always there for the taking. Ask for growth and you'll get it. Ask for art and you'll get that too. There are realms in the afterlife that strictly engage in matters of art, art in many expressions and forms. If you want to see great painters or musicians, it's all there. If you want to learn any one of the arts, the teachers and classes are there for you. Whatever it is that inspires you and opens your heart and the heart of others inspires the Divine. Please think of the artistic realm as an enormous community where there are universities, galleries, studios, archival libraries, museums, and workshops in every expression of art. There are also places where art is used to promote healing because art is an amazing tool that can help people work through their painful stories and unresolved past. So yes, there is definitely a place in the afterlife for all the artists of the world where they can master their craft and continue their personal and spiritual growth.

28

I keep repeating negative patterns that I can't get out of. Is my past the cause of all this negativity?

There is an unfortunate mainstream belief that says looking at our past is counterproductive, useless, and a waste of time. This kind of thinking is wrong and extremely dangerous to our mental and physical health. An unexamined life leads us all to misery because we end up repeating negative patterns over and over. Our history, which is our story, our personal story, is who we are and the narrative that has shaped us. To not look at our personal narrative is to not live our truth. We can't be fully anchored in our present when we don't have a grip on our past, and when we aren't anchored in the present, our future is at the mercy of unconscious and unhappy decisions. Set the intention to become aware and tackle the change that's going to put your life on track. It all starts with awareness. Once you set the intention, try to be truthful and honest about your past. Don't sugarcoat it. Everyone's life has some dark chapters. Find the truth and let yourself feel the loss, whatever the loss is: loss of innocence, aliveness, humor, individuality, joy, direction, strength, vulnerability, compassion, etc. You don't have to do this all alone. Look for a wise friend and or therapist to work through the dark chapters so you can come out on the other side where there is light.

We don't have to repeat our negative patterns, but we will if we avoid, deny, suppress, and distort the truth of our past. Your repetition of negative decisions will not stop until you heal the past wounds. Negative repetition is the soul's way of telling us that something is still not healed. We repeat the negative because the painful story that we buried is breaking through, and dark stories can't be buried forever. They'll break through and produce mental, emotional, financial, or physical breakdowns. They'll break through because the soul is pushing for growth, regeneration, transformation, and evolution and you can't do that without the truth of the past. You can get out of your negative patterns when you explore what events and experiences from the past shaped your present. Brave people find the review of their past exhilarating and liberating and end up reclaiming pieces of themselves that they had left behind. Don't be afraid to review the past. Do it with courage and honesty and know that God is beside you because God wants us all to live our truth and full potential and we can't live our full potential if the truth of the past is hidden from us.

As we grow into more emotional maturity, our spirituality deepens and helps us make sense of our history. Emotional growth and spiritual growth go hand in hand. To get out of the maze of the compulsion to repeat the negative, we must revisit the past and not see it as something to avoid and minimize. The jump to a healthy future happens when the past is at rest, at peace, in closure. To not revisit, review and resolve the past is to be stuck in a repetitive negative present and a foreboding future. Looking at the past with sincerity is one of the most productive things we can do for ourselves as well as one of the most rewarding. It's an opportunity to gather up the sacred pieces we once lost and a chance at a better life.

***

29

It's almost impossible for me to go back to the memories of my childhood because I can't remember anything under the age of nine. How do I reclaim my childhood memories?

The fact that you have memories after the age of nine is a good thing and a start. Start with a "memory journal" and write down whatever you do remember. You can also do a "memory art journal" if you are an artist. Work with a skilled therapist and start collecting and journaling all the pieces you do remember. Ask parents, relatives or adults who knew you as a child about their experiences with you or their stories about you. Your mental memory might be weak but the visceral is still there; it's always there. On a visceral level check what happens to your body when you think of mom, dad, brother, vacations, grandmother, school, playground, or teacher? Does your body feel fear, disgust, deadness, contraction, defense, rage, joy, numbness? You see the body houses the memory on a cellular and visceral level because the body doesn't forget. Work with someone who can take those body reactions and help you process and integrate them.

Go through old photo albums and observe your physical reactions to them. Go visit where you grew up if that isn't too disturbing to you. The mental system of a young person forgets so he can survive and not be flooded and overwhelmed by unpleasant thoughts and emotions. It's very likely that the emotions of the first nine years of your life were too difficult for your system to process so it chose amnesia. Or maybe something happened at nine that was too much for your senses. Talk to family members who might give you some of the missing pieces. Be a good detective. The amnesia helped you endure, survive, and go on to adulthood, so please don't see it as a negative or a terrible thing. What is important to reclaim is the joy and innocence of childhood, so if there are things in your life right now that bring you joy and great pleasure, pursue them. Those things that now give you joy will smooth over the pain of childhood and give meaning to your present.

For those who suffer from childhood amnesia the healing route can be through body awareness and self-expression. For example, if your body cringes and your throat locks up when you think of your grandmother, you have just collected a large piece of information about your childhood through the truth of your body. The body doesn't lie, and it will bring more and more waves of truth to surface if you stay with the process. The surfacing of the old material will free you from the pain of the past and slowly open up your memory. This will take time so be patient with yourself and your body. Memory can't be pushed to the surface by force. Respect the timing and rhythm of the body. Develop body sensitivity and get to know how your body reacts to different people and events. When we're with people we enjoy, our body relaxes, and our breathing opens up. Around people we don't feel safe with, our body contracts and changes in breathing and chemistry. As you continue to make this association between people from your childhood and your body reactions, you'll eventually have pieces of your history. If the mental memory apparatus has failed, the body can come to the rescue because all that happened in the past is recorded in the body. All emotions are networked and wired within the body. When we feel fear, pleasure, or desire, all those feelings are experienced inside the body. When you smell something that reminds you of your loving grandma, it's your body that responds and experiences the feelings of love and pleasure. When you see a leather belt and your body shivers and your mind goes blank, it's your body that is remembering. Find an astute healing practitioner who appreciates the body's wisdom and will work with your childhood amnesia through body awareness to promote your healing and recovery.

***

30

Does everyone in the afterlife experience growth and evolution?

Everyone is experiencing growth and evolution whether they know it or not. The criminal who has had twenty lives in criminality will one day feel the fatigue of being a criminal and change his ways. When he discovers that the criminal life doesn't bring about inner peace, he will look for a fresh start. Even when we are in a bad place, that bad place is going to take us to a place of awareness and healing one day. All roads lead to healing, eventually. All roads lead to inner peace and unity, all roads lead to God.

Everyone is in a healing process, everyone. For some, growth moves very very slow because they aren't reflective, and they carry a lot of defenses. Whether you're in the afterlife or the earth life you are growing even if you refuse to. You're growing because sooner or later you're going to hear the whisper or the scream of your inner self. It could take one year or hundreds of years, but you'll eventually reflect and change your ways. It takes a lot of energy to not change and hold on to defenses and distorted beliefs, a lot. Souls eventually experience fatigue from all that holding and surrender to their higher calling.

The afterlife, just like earth, offers enormous opportunities for growth and evolution but not everyone takes the offer, some would rather hang out and remain idle. If the afterlife was a place where all souls evolved and grew at rapid pace, we would have very few unaware souls coming into earth. In the afterlife, just like earth, the distractions away from growth are many. If souls want to occupy themselves with bad habits and refuse to grow, they can do that, free will applies. Although they may choose an idle existence, that doesn't mean they aren't growing. When an idle existence filled with negative pleasure fails to bring fulfillment to a soul after let's say a hundred lifetimes and a hundred visits to the afterlife, that soul will start looking around for meaning and choose to evolve. You see, you can't force someone into evolution, even in the afterlife. You can show them the way as the many teachers and guides do in the afterlife, but it's up to the soul to decide which road to take. The spiritual teachers and guides are very respectful of free will. They are evolved enough to know that all souls will eventually choose evolution and oneness with God. Ultimately, none of us can escape the wheels of evolution, we can only delay it. Evolution will patiently grind down our false ambitions and selfishness until we align ourselves to the heart centered will of a spiritual life. The soul's growth and evolution are sometimes rigidly slow but as experiences are accumulated, the soul eventually softens and blends with spiritual values and spiritual substance.

***

31

I'm a woman in my forties and my mother still disrespects my privacy. This happens to me at work too. What's going to take for things to change?

If people keep walking into your room without knocking who needs to change, you or them? Of course the answer is you because they may never change in this lifetime. You're the one who must speak up with courage and send a message that you won't tolerate behavior that goes against your grain and that you want your privacy respected. It's up to you to have a firm talk with them about their intrusion and maybe place a sign or a lock on the door so they can learn to honor your boundaries. We can't wait, wish, and hope that others change so we can have a happy life. We can and should pray for their change, but our focus should be on our change and growth. So how do you focus on your change and growth? It all starts with honesty, being honest about your strengths, fears, and shortcomings. Here what you need is the balance between your kindness and your assertion. When people are trampling on your kind heart, it's time to gather your strength and put up some defenses and protect your heart. It's also time to pray for some new friends who can become your spiritual brothers and sisters.

If you are attracting abuse into your life, then you'll have to look at why you're magnetizing that. If the people you know are violating your boundaries and disrespecting your space and opinions, it's time for change. The change is you. The strength inside you that has been hidden for years and put on the back shelf must come out. Set the intention to connect to your hidden strengths and invite them out. It takes time to get used to the new you, the you that possess firmness and decisiveness. At the core, our emotional journeys are about self-possession. A self-possessed person has access to the full spectrum of his emotions. He can feel anger as well as sorrow, he can say no as well as yes, he can be tender as well as firm. He has possession of all his feelings in a healthy and contained ego. His delivery is solid as well as compassionate. Find support groups in your community or a good therapist that will give you permission to say no. When you learn to say no then you'll make room to say yes to your privacy.

So, what feelings and emotions do you need to possess in order for others to respect your privacy? Just drop into your gut and pay attention and you'll know. Maybe you're afraid to hurt their feelings with your request for privacy or maybe it's too scary for you to ask for what you want. There are a number of reasons why this dynamic with your mother and coworkers is going on, and you can fix it. Bring it all back to yourself and do an honest self study and see what you come up with. The more honest you are the faster the solutions. Pray and work towards self-possession and you'll soon surround yourself with people who hear you and whom you enjoy.

***

32

Can criminals be reformed by spiritual healing?

We all need spiritual healing because we are all spiritual beings. Let's first define spiritual healing – the core of spiritual healing is the process of bringing someone closer to their longing for love and for God and to help them recognize that we are all one. When people are disconnected form their soulful purpose they live in separation and it becomes easy for them to steal, lie, or even kill. As spiritual healers, it's our obligation to recognize that criminals are more than their crime. They are souls who have the same aspirations as everyone else and the same need to express who they really are. But somewhere down the karmic line their expression got distorted and the forces that were supposed to support them didn't fully come through. Somewhere down the line the family, the friends, the relatives, if there were any, the teachers and the culture didn't fully deliver. It takes a broken village to produce a criminal.

The healing process for the criminal is to feel remorse and accountability but that's not going to stop crime. What will stop crime is when the leaders of a culture or community express remorse and accountability as well. The healing process must eventually be all inclusive, comprehensive, and socially holistic. Not only the criminal but also the warden, the guards, the mayor, the governor, the policymakers, the judges, the lawyers, and everyone that shapes and plays part in the criminal justice system can benefit from spiritual healing. You may reform one criminal but then how do the others flourish in a society where the privileged don't share power and resources? You see it isn't just about the criminal. Around the criminal is a large circle of issues such as housing, healthcare, job training, literacy, nutrition, and a perverted philosophy about selfishness and individualism. This last one is important to look at from a healing perspective because a philosophy that says everyone should be able to do it on their own creates chaos, separation, and disorder. So, we all need healing, not just the criminal. We need to gain a deeper insight into what forces in a culture promote criminal behavior and what preventive measures work. Placing criminals behind bars without repairing social and cultural ills won't heal the planet. Building more prisons is a lot more expensive than providing free or affordable college and vocational education. Paying for the salaries of wardens, prison administrators and guards is again a lot more expensive than providing healthcare for children. "We are our brother's keeper," and if we deny and reject this spiritual doctrine, we'll be building a lot more prisons and hiring a lot more wardens. Spiritual healing is the process of removing the veil of separation between people and recognizing that if we don't help each other, we all suffer. As long as one person is still suffering in your village, the job isn't done. For those who move and shake and shape culture in a negative way, the message to you is clear: please consider your spiritual healing journey. There's only one river and we're all in it.

***

33

What do you see for the future of the planet?

The future is about redefining power - what is powerful and what power is. The way power is discussed and displayed today has more to do with separation than connection. Real power doesn't ask questions like who has more and who's in control? It asks who is cooperating, sharing, and helping? Real power has to do with connecting, linking, unifying, merging, combining, bonding, and uniting. God will let you and I play around with our free will for a while but if our free will is pushing the envelope, God's going to step in and have Divine Will dictate; make no mistake about that because God will have the last word. It's like a parent who'll let you wonder about until you get in serious trouble. Well, we're in serious trouble so the plug on the men and women who have been misusing their leadership powers is getting pulled. God has been patiently watching and, in a few years, will be drawing the line, drawing the line means enough acting out. The planet is moving from the third chakra to the fourth, from power to heart. It has no more tolerance for powerful people acting out their personal childhood injuries through exploitation, violence, and greed. They have to get into therapy and if they refuse, therapy will be coming to their doorstep. This isn't about doom and gloom; it's simply about balancing the scales.

Those who have been disillusioned by the human race will soon find and feel hope because centuries of separation are coming to a close and a new era is approaching. The false pillars of the "me consciousness" are cracking and will collapse in the next two generations. No more what's in it for me without thinking and caring about the entire human race. Power will slowly but surely become anchored in the heart and to the heart it makes no sense to not share resources and information. Many evolved souls from the "we consciousness" have already incarnated to earth and are setting up the networks to connect, link and unify the globe in a big way, a very big way. We are moving toward a value-based expression of power whether we believe it or not. The many evolved children who have come to earth in the last twelve years are children who can't be pulled out of their center and heart and as they become the future leaders, which they will, they will realign the distribution of all resources - wealth, health, food, technology, education, and environment. For the next two hundred years, the rescue and care of the environment will be the top agenda for most countries and governments because of the enormous damage we have inflicted to our planet. This effort to care for and repair the environment and the planet will force global cooperation and greater unity, a unity that has never been seen before.

The future is very promising but there is work to be done and the best place to start is with the individual.

There is a saying that goes, "if you want to change the world, change your world." So, what is it that you need to change in your world? What are your personal soulful longings and passions? What will make you more spiritual? Clear your personal life and put things in order - forgive, look for a new job, fix the marriage, finish the degree, speak up, surrender to your grief, say no, and say yes to your Divine purpose. Do what it takes to change your world - read self help books, see a therapist, pray, heal your broken feelings, turn to God. As your world changes and becomes brighter and more colorful, you'll begin to see and feel hope for the world. You'll begin to look for a way, anyway, to make a contribution, a contribution that will give you meaning. The future is filled with billions of people making contributions, large and small contributions that will add up to a gigantic vortex of power that connects, links, unifies, merges, bonds and unites. The future is secure as long as you and I work on our personal stuff and focus on contributing something dear. If we don't purify our little world, we'll contaminate the world out there. All the powers that have exploited and lied will soon experience their humbling hour; it's inevitable because greed, self–interest, separation, arrogance, and evil are always and always on a collision course; by nature, they are entities that eventually self-destruct. In less than five years the shifts will start happening where the "me" based power will begin to slowly surrender to the heart-based power of the "we." It's all about balancing the energies and that's the spiritual future we're all walking into.

***